09025

ckaway, Catherine M., 1919-
iding into morning / Catherine Buckaway. --
skatoon : Thistledown Press, c1989.
4 p. : map.

987531   ISBN:0920633625 (pbk.)

North West Mounted Police (Canada) - Fiction. I. Title

Riding into Morning

iding into Morning

Catherine Buckaway

Thistledown Press

Canadian Cataloguing in Publication Data

Buckaway, Catherine M., 1919-

  Riding into morning

  Poems
  ISBN: 0-920633-62-5

1. North West Mounted Police (Canada) - Poetry.
I. Title.

PS8553.U352R5 1989 C811/.54 C89-098127-2
PR9199.3.B835R5 1989

Book design by A.M. Forrie
Cover art by Chris Armstrong
Typeset by Thistledown Press Ltd.

Printed and bound in Canada by
Hignell Printing Ltd., Winnipeg

Thistledown Press Ltd.
668 East Place
Saskatoon, Saskatchewan
S7J 2Z5

Acknowledgements

Map "The Whoop-Up Trail" from *Whoop-Up Trail: Early Days in Alberta-* [
Gerald L. Berry (Allied Art Products, 1953), used by permission of the aut
Berry.
Excerpt from "The March West" by S.W. Horrall from *Men in Scarlet* edite
A. Dempsey (Historical Society of Alberta/McClelland and Stewart West, 1
by permission of the Historical Society of Alberta. © Historical Society of
Excerpt from "Whoop-Up Trail, International Highway of the Great Plai
E. Sharp (*Pacific Historical Review*, 1952) used by permission of the U
California Press. © University of California Press.
Excerpts from *Fort Whoop-Up* by Georgia Green Fooks, Whoop-Up Count
Historical Society of Alberta, used by permission of the Lethbridge Histori
© City of Lethbridge.

This book has been published with the assistance of The Canada Coun
Saskatchewan Arts Board.

To the Kinsmen Foundation,
thanks for the electronic typewriter

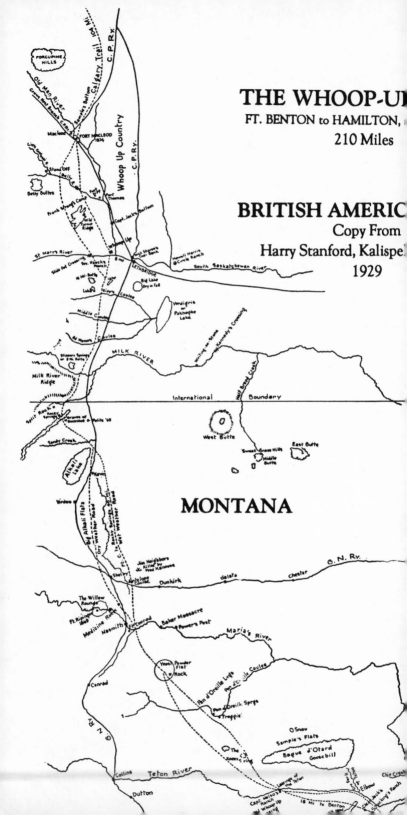

THE WHOOP-U[P]
FT. BENTON to HAMILTON,
210 Miles

BRITISH AMERIC[A]
Copy From
Harry Stanford, Kalispe[ll]
1929

MONTANA

We are walking; as men always walked
and I can feel my body made strong
out of muscles and bones, and my father
beside me, a togetherness of spirit.
The pride in him is made
of home and soil. A welding of sky and wind—
touching the nourished earth. And I,
Frank Arnot, wear sun in my eyes,
a whole world before me and only twenty-two.
Tomorrow I will begin my journey West.

A LETTER TO JANIE

When I leave this country
I will see your face—
but I am grown beyond you.
Your mother wants
us to be wed
though life weaves different things.
Gentle voice I will leave
your love behind;
retain in memory
the scent of sun
on your white limbs—
your hair caught on light,
your laughter
a bird's wing in sky.
The old familiarities gone.
A sacred trust   your
virtue—still untouched,
I go now to hide
from my heart.

June 6th, 1874

It begins with the gathering at Toronto.
You join the police   highly uniformed,
and the journey just started.
And you in the long wail of the train
jostling from the station.
The skirts of women drag like
wounded stars on the platform
newly planked. And the loneliness...
the taste of blood—voices fragment
in the thunder of the train.
I am going back to where I've always lived
for I am a farmer with love of land
veiled strongly in stillness deep-ingrained.

THE PRAIRIE

Train threads
shape back
rails' tongue
gathering voice
from destiny

and heart pumps
in solemn rhythm
over land
bare and brown

nurturing seeds
of scarlet
purpose and season
wedged from life
into one great distance
to Fargo

and ravelled
days
like dragonflies
on waters furred
with gold
weave songs

a march
into gauze
of raven wind
as sky and prairie
swallow each other
at Dufferin

n order to save time, arrangements were made to ransport the second contingent to Manitoba by ail through the United States to Fargo, North Dakota. From here it would march north to Fort Dufferin, the starting point for the expedition, where it would be joined by the first group of men already at Lower Fort Garry.

"The March West", S.W. Horrall, in *Men in Scarlet,* edited by Hugh A. Dempsey, Historical Society of Alberta/McClelland and Stewart West.

Somewhere in our flesh
sweet flowing blood—
but not enough
to warm our liquid bones.
Night burns heat from the prairie
for a thousand miles beyond
the stars that seed it.

★   ★

On the night of our arrival
at Dufferin, a dreadful storm,
and men weary of travel
knew the whip of rain—
a maelstrom of lightning and thunder,
and horses stampeded at midnight,
knocking over the wagons
that surrounded them.
A time that turned upon itself.
Some men were trampled,
and mules ran at full speed—
the spiced task
of rounding the creatures up.
A fifty mile travesty
of exhaustion   bewildered by the darkne
and lost upon the prairie.

★   ★

Good fortune let us gain the horses;
their freshness lost
on the long trek from Fargo—
and only one man drowned
in the swollen waters
of the Pembina River.

We smiled then
a marriage of true hearts
and the sun was dreaming.
Arms and ammunition,
saddlery and harness and general stores
were served out,
and packed in wagons and oxcarts.

★   ★

The prairie echoed with the sound
of hooves, the harsh voices
of the men, the bombardment
of hard work, a diminishment
of spirit stumbling
on rocks and horse droppings.

The food was bad,
and caught within their needs
men deserted   emptying the ranks.
And then a substitute of fifty men—
a patchwork quilt of lives
hopeful to belong to the West.

★   ★

And still no blood spilled
only our scarlet tunics
billowed out a sort of message;
and the grog shops
revamped our spirits—
rum in thick cups
yanked our gullets
to meet the crushed shell
of our thirst . . . laughter wrenched
from the misgiving day,
splintering the crumbling hours,
the bite and flake of a new land.

Whisky traders were a serious menace to the Baker and Power companies during the early years. Their unscrupulous traffic kept the Indians in a constant state of excitement which led to frequent disturbances. Indian wrath kindled by whisky traders often fell upon the legitimate traders as well. Intoxicated Indians visited Baker Posts, menacing the traders with ugly threats and throwing the trading into hopeless confusion. Colonel S.C. Ashley recorded the threats of one spirited brave: 'You miserable dirty white dog. You are here with your cattle eating our grass, drinking our water, and cutting our wood. We want you out of here, or we will wipe you out.'

"Whoop-Up Trail, International Highway on the Great Plains", Paul F. Sharp, *Pacific Historical Review*.

Indian atrocity reports,
of traders with hands and feet
cut off and hung from trees,
filled our mouths and everyone
discouraged   not knowing
what to do about them.
We do not want to believe
or dare not that they are true.

★   ★

Running against a tide
of wind and days thickened
and hacked with screeching
frenzy of the Red River carts.
Wheels and axles break
and wagons unplanked—
oxen strain, their strength mythical
beneath the crows' sudden cries.
Cows and calves waddle in the prairie mi
and still the column moves.

Uniforms, the colour of blood,
catching sunlight   three hundred of the
an existence within existence.
Riders unused to saddles—
a laboured joke   a snatch of song.

★   ★

Bison keep their difficult balance
a bonding of bone and sinew,
so many, brown like autumn leaves—
their breath rasping in a way
men have forgotten. Their
short, curved horns—powder flasks.
Pemmican from the Indians—
sweetened with marrow and berries,
and hides smoke-stunned—
steel-heeled hooves—the tips of arrows.
And the prairie a tangle of willows.
Wolves howl for rations thrown away.

Our guide, the French Métis,
Pierre Léveillé, thick-planted in the earth,
an interpreter curled around
fertile Indian languages
like a winding sheet.
A mountain of muscle and bone—
a lineage of giants—
his eyes eagle-winged—
riding a horse larger
than anyone can remember.

★   ★

Men, unused to Indian ways,
lured to abandoned camps
seek where quick brown hands
have left arrows and flints—
souvenirs among the hawkweed—
ancient excrement or bits of fur
and lice their only prize
itching like sandpaper
beneath their high-ringed collars.

★   ★

One by one   mowing machines,
wheels shaken in the pull and pall
of hidden stones break down.
To the Blackfoot scouts
who crouch and trail us,
these toebone wastes that
lie abandoned on the plain,
tell chiefs of our madness—
all these riches open to the sun.

★   ★

The Indians stay well out of sight,
not a single one,
we ride into the morning;
horses' hooves tapping away
the edges of the prairie.
Heat and dust cut our nostrils,
and men, rife with dysentery,
ride on calloused rumps—
each face a new fresh wound
from bites of flies and mosquitoes.

★   ★

Métis oxdrivers smirk—
their dark bright eyes
hammer us like wolves
when we cry out for
drinkable water.
They work their own strange ways
each separate driver gossiping
deep into our flesh.

BLACKSMITH

Where are the women I used to know?
Surely not in this place
where coyotes start howling at dusk.
Somehow I've survived this long
and freezing discipline;
unravelled the months into knotted arms.
Throat-veins thickened in a kind of pride
of physical action. I ply my trade
with tongue of fire—bronze-fisted—
jacketless—a dumb directedness,
the only thoughts drinkable water
and the soft noses of horses.
Surely there must be another
and easier promised land
and no place to go but West.

SOLDIER

In truth my wife
was a tyrannical shrew;
tongue stinging
the shutters of my eyes.
Not one for work,
carrying words like vultures
to the neighbours.
I lied and called myself single
to join this Force.
Let her scrabble-dirt
brothers support her.

In secret I am still
a rookie caught
in the language of the plains—
I can only remember shadows
of grain crops growing.
I wear like amulets
the thread of days;
I cannot unkey my feelings
nor believe I have
crossed this distance.

I was a soldier
now turned police.
Heavy with survival
I have nightmares still.
The others laugh
but I think they are
affected by my screams.
I've spilled blood
that flares my mind
and carries in the hard air
a night-hawk edge of pain.

One night the sky is lit
with a prairie fire out of control
that turns the grass
sideways into ashes,
and every second breath
is windwafted in the hating air.
Now ashes rise like clouds
and in the long miles shake
not a drop of water
to disentangle thirst,
and grey-black earth
is motionless   unmoved.
Horror grips our guts
until we reach the waving grass
and hope threads our veins.

★   ★

At dawn we yawn ourselves awake
to grasshoppers drumming on our tents—
a bitter spray of insects
with mouths as sharp as glass
covering everything in sight
with demonic energy
furrows of sound—
a beginning of insanity.
At this moment we feel nothing
but anger and pack our tents.
The insects gnaw our uniforms
and pit our carbine butts,
then rise like eagles
bellying in the full wind
around all other sound.

★   ★

We go where the Indians go
and the buffalo. Not an easy task.
Our only companions
are wind and sun.
Guts swell from alkali water
for we are not west-wise
and hours spear themselves
upon hours, and stomachs groan
from steer meat fresh-slain,
not given time to cool.
Gun butts catch on limbs
and each breath a darkness.

★   ★

Fifty of our horses, eastern-bred,
sicken on the ragged edges
of the prairie grass—
emaciated and weak,
and the wind in the sage
names death, but
only a few die   left
for wolves to feast on.
Life leans on the others,
their bones used mainly
for skin to lean on.

★   ★

Sixteen days have gone
and two hundred and seventy miles
out of Dufferin,
each mile slashed
with sun flames and everyone
accounted for. The scent of water
cuts our nostrils, and French
chooses a site by the Souris River.
We freely laugh
and slough trail dust
from our bodies. The river
moves with men—shapes imprinted
in the water's shadows.
Animals feast on the satin lining
of the lush grass. A rejuvenation
of men and creatures.

Colour of sky
current breathes
the prairie

> *white-tailed deer*
> *elusive as elves*
> *leap from thickets*

buffalo tithed in blood
gnaw minutes
from the flutes of day

> *gentle hills*
> *wear green-fire*
> *gowns*

sundrops like rainbows
on parchment water

> *shadows shape*
> *the river's edge*
> *as day dims*

night breezes
brush the campfires
free from memories
seeded in the stars

> *the world*
> *changes*
> *to fold back*
> *unbidden Time*

Everything on the prairie moves but us.
Deer, their muscles quivering,
speed over stones and grass.
Still we rest
bone-weary   men are sick.
Sky, laced with ducks and geese,
carries its message towards autumn.
So we wait until Colonel French
decides what to do . . . the fear of winter
on the open plains crumbles
the corners of his sun-baked mouth.

☆   ☆

It had been intended
that we stay together
until we reach the Rockies—
where the wind blows
through the silver trees
and mountains nudge the sky.
Now every ruined moment speaks
of danger and we must not
linger here. The column must be
divided   reduced in size.
Its length shortened,
divested of the slow-moving
carts and wagons.

☆   ☆

It is decided that Inspector Jarvis,
a lean tough man in charge of A troop,
will go to Fort Edmonton.
'Good men,' he says.
'They never let me down.'
We will reach Fort Edmonton
before the winter comes.
Unyoked oxen that loll at the river's edge
are yoked again, the sickest horses cut loose.
They went, harness and boots
worn thin. They will reach
the fort three months later
and no man lost
with horses fattened into winter.
They fought their way twelve hundred miles
of charcoal-green, passing beneath
the dissolving skies   subsisting
on bannock baked on black-spruce sticks,
and pemmican as hard as nails
that darken in the northern air.

★   ★

We stay five days
beside the Souris, the carts repaired
and horses freshened, and all the while
we spread ourselves upon the river's bank
With spirits raised, we turn
north from the border
and for the moment   a time of magic.
It does not last, and troubles crouch
in grass that rabbits cannot nibble.
Grasshoppers flail the land
and long strands of hunger
thumb-spreads our food—
pemmican made from the hooves
and horns of buffalo
everyone discouraged or so we say .

☆   ☆

The horses stumble onward
and grain is low and nothing
to cheer us. Only lone Indians
on horseback, and those far-off,
vanish before we reach them.
No hordes of painted warriors
to break the boredom of our hours.
The dried dung of buffalo everywhere.
As before, the oxen plod
like old men whose days
float across the void of life,
lag sometimes a day
behind our column, their
carefree drivers indifferently
cheering each other and shouting
obscenities at the unyielding plain.

☆   ☆

We meet a small band of Indians,
a handful of men in rags
and tatters with nothing
alive in their eyes—
their hair feathers loose and falling,
and braids   lice-ridden.
Sioux from south of the Medicine Line
seeking the Great Queen's protection,
their tears like perspiration
on the skulls of ancient gods.
And French, his heart moved
with compassion, gives them food
and tobacco. The column moves on
while hawks sun-tipped soar overhead.

The Cypress Hills are in an isolated position in the otherwise bald and uninspiring prairie. It seems as though, when God was building the western reaches of North America, the hills were thrown up or together in a whimsical mood to confuse mankind and excite his curiosity.

Fort Whoop-Up, Georgia Green Fooks, Whoop-Up Country Chapter, Historical Society of Alberta

It is the latter part of August
as we approach the Cypress Hills.
To the southwest, legions
of jutting landscape
wind and unwind, grounded
in earth   appendages
forever twisted into madness.
But the grazing is better
and buffalo signs appear—
one old bull shot
iron-fleshed and almost inedible.
Then three days later   more buffalo,
their flesh bearing the sweetness
of sage and willows.
The men eat contentedly,
their bellies filled   appetites sated,
glad high cycles of laughter
in the thin sun.

This meat is tough enough to break the jaws of an alligator.

It should be. It was a cayak buffalo.

What's a cayak buffalo?

An old buffalo kicked out of the herd by the young bucks and never allowed to return to it.

Cayak or not, he was all horns and hooves. The sonofabitch deserved to be put out of his misery.

I hope all buffalo meat ain't this tough.

No. I've eaten it before and found it tender and sweet to the taste.

One hell of a life. Alkali water that stinks like horse shit and ruins my guts.

Pemmican made of hooves and horns and mixed I think with slough grass instead of berries.

No glamour left in the scarlet uniform now.

No way. I've saddle sores and my horse has bronco ancestry.

Just once more to hear a woman's voice, a drink of whisky and a soft bed to sleep in.

Forget it. You're a policeman now.

A lost police, I don't think our leaders know where we are.

Yeah. We're lost. I guess they'll pick our b
off the prairie next spring.

Quit being such a pessimist. I'd settle for
drink of rum.

You'll settle for alkali coffee and be damn
glad of it.

I'm tired of it all.

I know. I feel the same way.

If there was any place to go I'd take off. E
scared of Indians.

You've got a yellow streak right down you

Shut up. Let's go catch rabbits and have r
stew for supper.

Some of the men set rabbit snares
and skinned the rabbits
all but the heads;
hands wiped free of blood and guts
hold the stench of a slaughterhouse,
and only a handful of the meat
is culled from the bones—
and the dead eyes
of the animals
squirm and sizzle on the open fires.

The night shadows
smooth,   and moonlight
weaves its magic
over this wild land.

★   ★

All the time now we pass
through buffalo herds
hunchbacked   shambling—
their hooves dig great holes
in the grass and the horses starve.
A night of freezing rain
kill nine of them and time
spins backward into our
slackening flesh.
And half of us, to spare the animals,
walk; and the land sharpens underfoot.

☆   ☆

Even the oxen   tough-bred,
stumble into bruised death,
and stripped of their yokes
lie stiff and cold.
Wind strings greenly over them
and crows pick their upturned eyes.
In grime and sweat our route
swings southward now
to the Sweet Grass Hills—
our horses falling again and again
to reach this place we've never been.
Then sun breaks the dawn
and once more the grazing is good.

Alone in the dark I dreamed
last night of Janie
whose breasts—fragile as moonbeams—
held the scent of roses;
silk skirts billowed against
her honey thighs. In my dream
I felt their warmth.
I awoke so hurt with desire
my cheeks drowned in tears.
Beneath these different stars
love soft as breathing
is discarded on
a cold shore of regret
that threads my trembling heart.

FREDERICK BAGLEY   TRUMPETER

I leave Old Buck, my horse,
chewing the sweet juice stems
that flesh him into sleekness.
I am the youngest, just sixteen,
and I go wandering alone
in this Sweet Grass land.
Curiosity pulls me into caves
that hold no sun.
Upon their rounded walls
pictographs wrenched from life—
older than man's first words
animals   birds   myths.
In the language of the dead
I hear each separate
echoing from the shadows
of the West Butte,
and realize sadly that no one
dwells here anymore.

In final division,
two troops leave us
carrying sunlight
on their lean and arching backs,
their horses leaner still—
phantom men on phantom horses;
their destination Fort Pelly
near the Manitoba border.
Heartbeats govern heartbeats
with strength leaked out;
but they transcend
two thousand miles
incredibly efficient
on the green-fisted plain.

JOURNEY TO FORT BENTON

September 22, 1874

We leave the others at Cripple Camp
to renew themselves and rendezvous
at the Whoop-Up Trail. If only
he could see me now. I wear
the Queen's scarlet and ride to Fort Benton
and wind and sun and pride
flow into one for I am chosen
to go with French. I remember
my father's disappointment in me.
An early pulling of resentment,
and companions no better than
they should be—leaving work undone
and he shouldering the extra tasks.
Liquor the colour of amber—
the raucous days—the nights unslept
and sadness pulsing in his veins.

The wind turns cold
and summer birds
nurtured in a globe of sky
prepare for their journey south.
We ride south as well,
our breath licking the miles.
Wolves scream in the night,
and moon tilts like feathered bones
through the ravelled hours.
And not one Indian,
we are most fortunate
for they hate the white man
in this different land.
Then Benton at last
and merchants unroll a welcome—
forbidden whisky as sweet as honeycomb
heats our bellies—a chuckling time
that folds back remembered hardships.

☆   ☆

Credit and supplies are arranged
through Ottawa   winter food
and clothing assured and horses,
shattered by exhaustion
replaced with new ones
as sturdy as the West
that bred them. Then French is
ordered back to Swan River,
and we lose this sure-languaged man;
his bravery untarnished
who led us for faceless miles
of primeval wilderness—
loss lies bitter on our tongues.

★   ★

Assistant-Commissioner Macleod
takes over command;
ranking north of Benton
our column of bull teams
and new mounts surrender
everything to the miles ahead—
with Jerry Potts, our guide
and interpreter.
This man wears for good luck
against his heart
a cat's skin turned inside out—
plain wise, his eyes wide-focused,
he counts the hours
to the call of rivers and plains.
A legend strung into history.

☆   ☆

Our journey is easier now;
although we spread ourselves for trouble
for we have orders to capture Fort Whoop Up.
No Blackfoot bother us
for Potts is their friend,
crafty in the knowledge
of a dozen tribal languages,
short in speech and never weary.
Miles flake away in the wind
weather fine   hunting and grazing
fat and sufficient
and sunlight an azure mirror.

☆   ☆

It is evening and October
flames across the land;
on the hill overlooking Fort Whoop Up
our hearts pound at the formidable scene
But only a silent American flag
moves on the bastion.
This place where stilled water
steeped in alcohol and gunpowder
was traded
to the Indians for furs
lies almost emptied of life;
only one old white man
dwells here now.
No warrior or trader he
rather a lover
four bronze-face women
keep him company.

Dave Akers is a lucky sonofabitch.

Four women for one man and us without any.

What does it matter if they're not white. I like the tall one myself.

Forced...celibacy.

Aw stop talking like a professor.

I was one, so I can talk as I like.

You'd better not mess with me.

Keep it down or the officers will hear you.

I bet they feel the same way.

I don't know. I still prefer a white woman.

I would like to try a bronze one, especially the little young one.

Some battle we were in.

Battle of Fort Whoop-Up.

Yeah. Invited for supper instead.

The grub is good. I'd forgotten what it's like to eat a woman's cooking.

Still it's not the same as at home.

We're not home now.

And we're not out of danger yet.

HE TAKES A MOUTHFUL OF VENISON.

Look at him, for a professor he eats a lot.

Oh quit picking on him. You're jealous yo
haven't got his education.

I'm not jealous.

Yes, you are.

Sh-sh. Here comes an officer.

THE MEN LAPSE INTO SILENCE.

We are on the move again,
the ever-present threat of winter
threads our minds.
Through long wind-swept grasses
in a land fat with buffalo,
elk and deer we follow Potts.
As the miles trace behind us
our spirits soar, our voices lift
in songs. Then the Oldman River,
a hospitable sight, reflects the sunset.
In the light of the jewel-pressed campfire
we gorge on buffalo haunch
and know our journey's ended.

ALIEN LOVE

Although Macleod has forbidden it
the call of flesh is strong   a primal need;
sexual abstinence wars with my hot blood
I sneak from camp and find her
amid the scent of wood-smoke—
the mint of stone fire-rings,
this woman of the wilderness.
All autumn falls on me,
for she is beautiful—
her hair—a midnight sheen
her eyes—the blackness of ebony.
Beneath her brown touch the aching
glory of my need finds blessed release;
I pour my seed into this alien flesh.
Afterwards, our passion spent,
we feast on nuts and berries
that hold the sweetness of a summer past.
Then patient as no other lover can be
she watches me as I return to camp.

But not our work, for now we build
Fort Macleod amid the cottonwoods
and wind that webs our river island.
Tents and horse lines up, we strip
to undershirts to toil with saws.
Broadaxes flatten timbers
and square them evenly to fit—
close-knit—before the real flow of winter.
We trench the rooted ground,
a stockade takes form
out of twist and gloss of wilderness;
and all the while the Blackfoot watch us.

★   ★

The Indians think us strange
young men   no women
to wash and cook for us;
but Potts explains
we are the Great White Mother's men
who have come to destroy
the whisky trade.
As the fort assumes its shape
minor chiefs of the Peigans and Bloods
visit. Macleod shares a full deer roasted
for they are incredible eaters.
He shares a pipe and syrup-thick
coffee and talks of peace.
Dark eyes glitter
words throb and pull—
a grudging respect is born
for this eagle white man.

WHISKY RECIPES

Whisky
Painkiller Medicine
Hostetter's Bitters
Castile Soap
Blackstrap Chewing Tobacco
Colour with red ink and serve hot

One quart whisky
One pound chewing tobacco
Handful of red pepper
One bottle of Jamaica ginger
One quart of molasses
Dash of red ink

1 gallon of high wine
3 gallons of water
1 quart of alcohol
1 pound of black chewing tobacco
1 handful of red peppers
1 bottle of Jamaica ginger
1 quart black molasses
Water *ad libitum*
Mixed well and boiled until the strength is drawn
from the tobacco and peppers.

1 keg of alcohol
2 cups of Perry's Painkiller
Hostetter's Bitters
Red ink
Castile Soap
Blackstrap Chewing Tobacco
Water

Alcohol
Florida water
Painkiller
Tobacco
Blue Stone

Fort Whoop-Up, Georgia Green Fooks, Whoop-Up
Country Chapter, Historical Society of Alberta

Our patrols ride the wilds
and every wagon searched
and whisky is torn away to join
the waters of the river;
honest traders set up
stores on the hill above the fort
a street appears where none has been befo
New friendships forged
peace slumbers on the snow-fed land.

★   ★

December 1, 1874

First whisper of December
and Crowfoot, the great Blackfoot chief,
intends to visit.
It is as good a reason as any
to wear our scarlet tunics;
equipment shines like light
against the azure sky.
He comes at last
with several lesser chiefs,
an eagle's wing in his hand
for he seeks peace.
Words of wisdom rise as soft
as the first sweet scent of snowflakes—
a final pact is sealed.
A gold-entangled miracle
takes root upon the plains.

JERRY POTTS, AS AN INTERPRETER TO THE POLICE, DESCRIBES IN HIS SUCCINCT WAY HOW THE NATIVES FEEL ABOUT THE NWMP

Several prominent chiefs were in attendance at Fort Macleod. Col. Macleod who had learned a few words of Blackfoot, recognized 'naki-okee' as whisky and 'napi-kwan' for 'white man' and rightly guessed that the chiefs were expressing their gratitude to the Mounted Police for ridding their hunting grounds of the whisky traders. Potts said nothing but upon being asked, he shrugged his shoulders and commented simply, 'Dey damn glad you're here.'

Fort Whoop-Up, Georgia Green Fooks, Whoop-Up Country Chapter, Historical Society of Alberta.